The Joy of Preaching
Encountering Jesus through the Word of God

Dr. James McReynolds

Minister of Joy to the World

The Joy of Preaching
Encountering Jesus through the Word of God

Dr. James McReynolds

Minister of Joy to the World

Parson's Porch Books

The Joy of Preaching

ISBN: Softcover 978-1-936912-70-4

Copyright © 2013 by James McReynolds

All rights reserved. No part of this book may be reproduced or transmitted in any form or by any means, electronic or mechanical, including photocopying, recording, or by any information storage and retrieval system, without permission in writing from the publisher.

Parsons Porch Books is an imprint of Parson's Porch & Company (PP&C) in Cleveland, Tennessee. PP&C is an innovative non-profit organization which raises money by publishing books of noted authors, representing all genres. All donations from contributors and profits from publishing are shared with the poor.

To order additional copies of this book, contact:

Parson's Porch Books

1-423-475-7308

www.parsonsporchbooks.com

This book is dedicated to everyone

who has heard my preaching and

has responded to the Word of God

Contents

First Forward by Harold Bales	9
Second Forward by Catherine Stander	12
Introduction	15
The Joy in the Calling	19
The Joy in the Preparation	26
Encountering Jesus in the Word of God	31
The Cross of Giving Something Good Every Time	39
Putting the Word of God into Human Words	57
Preaching for People Who Want to Go Back to Egypt	68
The Way of the Cross Leads Home	76
Preaching Joy and the Coming Kingdom	87
Preaching and the Conversion of the Soul	95
Why Bother With Preaching in the Church Today?	101
About the Author	117

Foreword

James McReynolds has been my friend for more than 40 years.

He and I first met when we were young staff members for our denominations—he a Southern Baptist and I a Methodist. We were both working in communication—he a Southern Baptist and I for the Methodist Board of Evangelism. We were both pursuing doctoral studies at the Vanderbilt University Divinity School in Nashville, Tennessee. He was born to be a communicator. More than this, he was born to be a preacher.

I have never known a person more extravagantly laden with endearing qualities that one would admire in a friend. Loyal to a fault, Jim maintains very close relationships with colleagues and friends over a lifetime. He keeps in touch. He is true to his calling.

He is ecumenical in spirit and moves easily among church denominations and among all kinds of people. He has a vibrant personality and joy is the theme of his life. "Amen" is not just a word at the end of a prayer; it is also a description of a life of affirmation. Jim McReynolds is an "Amen" person in the service of the Lord.

Jim is also a writer. It is sometimes said of prolific writers: "He or she never had an unpublished thought." This may be true of this good man. He has a demonstrated capacity to put the pen to paper that amazes a mere mortal. It is almost as if the injunction to "pray without ceasing" was, when it came to Jim, accompanied by an added footnote" "Write without ceasing too!" When the Lord called Jim McReynolds to preach, he also put a pen in his hand. And we are all the better for it.

I hope and expect that this book will not be his last. But, he is unlikely to ever write another that will be a more obvious hymn from his heart than this. He is foremost a preacher at heart and his is a state-of-the-art. He loves God and he loves people and everything else about him is commentary. If you are a veteran preacher you will identify with his book. If you are a young preacher you will learn from it. If you are wrestling with God's call to become a preacher, you may be nudged toward a "yes" by it. If you are a lay person and want to know what makes a preacher tick, you will get lots of insight into that here. Above all else, you will sense the joy of a preacher's soul here.

Jim McReynolds is a model of Christian character and ministerial faithfulness. He has demonstrated in his life's work his abiding faith in the character of God. Every page of this excellent book is

The Joy of Preaching

a testimony to the spirit of one who made the message of The Good Book come alive through his preaching to the people in the pews. I thank God for it.

Harold Bales

March 2013

Second Foreword

For my friend, encourager, and colleague in Christ, Jim McReynolds

About 15 years ago, I received my calling from God to become a preacher of the Word and it scared me to death. But like Isaiah, after the "Woe is me," I said, "Here am I, Lord." A few year later I was blessed to meet Jim, a very kind and compassionate man with a love for preaching the Word of God.

There are weeks when I am tired and worn, and the last "joyful" thing I feel like doing, is writing a sermon, but, I remember Jim and his joy for being chosen to preach God's Word and after seeking for forgiveness, I am lifted up and find it a joy to preach.

I owe this to God first and then to Jim who God placed in my path. Jim has a heart for Christ and not just for pulpit preaching, but for going out and sharing the Good News of Christ and bringing the

The Joy of Preaching

Light of Christ to the least of these, and he is a blessing to me and many others.

Jim and I work together in ministering to the outcast and the addicted as well as those with mental illness. Jim is a compassionate man who has taught me much and had faith in me, when I did not have any in myself, and I am forever grateful.

Jim also has a sense of humor which I cherish! Jim becomes discouraged as all of us ministers do from time to time. But, we lift each other up in prayer and then Jim writes another book in a week, like this one. Me, I go fishing! Oiy Vey!

I know you will find this book encouraging and uplifting!

Catherine A. Stander

March 2013

Introduction

SUMMER CAMP WAS ALWAYS A HIGHLIGHT of my church involvement. In 1954, I went to a Royal Ambassador Camp in Erwin, Tennessee with Jerry Brown, Doug Lewis, James Oldham, Bobby Fleming, Harry Lee Bowling, David Clark, Larry Odum, and some other boys who attended Woodlawn Baptist Church in Bristol, Tennessee.

We joined with boys from churches in the Holston Baptist Association in East Tennessee. Bible studies, preaching, swimming, ball games, prayer, and the things that make up a Baptist summer camp were enjoyed toward the last day, they held an evangelistic worship service designed to challenge boys to profess Christ as their Lord and Savior. Also, speakers asked if any of us felt a call to preach.

In most years, scores would go down front during the invitation to be saved, to rededicate their lives, or be called to a church vocation. Only one boy answered the call. That boy was me.

James McReynolds

A call to preach, in Baptist understanding, meant a call to become a pastor of a church. We called our pastor "preacher." From before my birth, my mother thought her son might become a preacher. As a little child, I played church. My playmates and I would create a church with boxes and things.

I always was the "preacher." Bob Fleming was the minister of music. Bob later went to seminary and became a wonderful music minister.

By age eight, I professed my faith in Jesus and was baptized by immersion. I read my King James Bible every day. In summer I'd go down to the basement and lay on the cold concrete floor to escape the heat.

By age 12 I was preaching. My first sermon (besides children's sermons) was titled, "Sermon Preached on a Football Field" from Matthew 6:33.

The message was preached on the field in front of Tennessee High School in Bristol before a football game between Haynesfield School and the church youth mission group, the Royal Ambassadors.

This book is one preacher's rich experience, the personal complemented by the communal, always the preacher in the context of the congregation. Share my itinerary as a preacher

The Joy of Preaching

through the call to preaching, my joy and my dread as I tried to speak for God.

Joy is the thread that holds my work together. Preaching is the joy of speaking of what we love to whom we love. My style has been informed by homiletics masters such as John Killinger, George Buttrick, David Buttrick, Barbara Taylor, Fred Craddock, Eugene Lowry, and Henry Mitchell.

One of my favorite English professors at Carson-Newman College told me that I had "a poetic soul, a gift of working language into something beautiful and meaningful." Agnes Hull was my teacher and a friend. She introduced me to Dr. Charles Trentham and the First Baptist Church in Knoxville with whom I served as student pastor for prayer. The Word of God has become flesh with God in my heart. Preaching is hard work. Preachers prepare to preach by dwelling with the Word through lectio divina, reading the text, struggling with it, responding to it in the preacher's own life, discussing it with parishioners and colleagues, reading the original Hebrew and Greek texts, reading commentaries, and clarifying the passage slowly, chewing on it as a cow chews its cud. Most of my insights can be applied to any setting. For the joy of preaching cannot be limited to Sundays in a local church sanctuary.

We must re-think church and take our preaching to the campus, the prison, hospital, community groups, and nursing homes.

James McReynolds

My favorite professor at Vanderbilt University Divinity School in Nashville was John Killinger. Hundreds of preachers owe their skill to Dr. Killinger, who could teach in a way that enabled each student to create his own style, gently causing preachers to rethink what it means to preach.

In ordination ceremonies, those called to be preachers receive a Bible and are told "take thou authority." By faithful preaching of the Word of God, the preacher reveals people's souls to themselves, gives them the power to make judgments that liberate them, and gives them confidence, certainty, and joy, which hell itself cowers.

For people in pain, the preacher can make a drastic difference. The only antidote for addictions, aimlessness, and agony is Jesus who brings light to darkness.

People found the joy of the Lord in the preaching of the apostle Peter, who had been transformed by the grace of Christ. In Peter, they found an authority in which they entrusted their lives. They could discover joy in their lives in a meaningful, transforming way.

The joy of preaching is not limited to Sundays in a church building. Those who have come to understand the promise and gift of preaching will find it as a means of grace, and always will find that it is an occasion for joy.

Chapter One
THE JOY IN THE CALLING

IN THE RECORD OF JEREMIAH'S CALL, GOD said, "Before I formed thee in the belly I knew thee; and before thou camest forth out of the womb I sanctified thee, and I ordained thee a prophet unto all nations." (Jeremiah 1:5)

What a mystery that God should call ordinary humans to speak the Word of God. This divine spiritual gift creates a sense of who the preacher is and who God is. This calling is initiated by God and the called must speak for God.

Isaiah said, "Woe is me! For I am undone; because I am a man of unclean lips, and I dwell in the midst of a people of unclean lips: for mine eyes have seen the King, the Lord of hosts. (Isaiah 6:5)

The preacher's immediate response to God may be an overwhelming sense of the limitations rather than a delightful awareness of being favored with a divine visitation.

A call to preach will set a young person up for public scrutiny and ridicule. So the young called ones can get unsettled in the depths of their beings.

Even in school, they are treated differently. Those talented enough to do most anything choose to do something mysterious that is not understood the same way as those who prepare to be physicians, lawyers, scientists, politicians, and those kind of jobs that are valued in today's society more than the value of a minister of the Word.

But that vision from God that accompanies the call to preach is so awesome and so compelling that it overrides the fear. The call may bring an initial sense of dread, but it also unleashes the inner urge to do what God desires.

Isaiah was so moved by the holiness, mystery, and glory of God that he said "Here am I, send me." If a human senses the glory of the Lord, rough treatment from one's peers and others is a small price to pay for one day to feel that glory again. Every call is personal. Some receive a fuzzy awareness, but even a limited sense of the health-giving Word of God is more compelling than anything else.

The Joy of Preaching

During the spiritual journey those called gain a realization that God requests them to speak his Word, and that request ignites sparks of fire and joy as expectation and creation of "the joy of the Lord."

The more the preacher is aware of the awesome request, the more the preacher makes reference to it and allows it to form his conception of preaching. "Truth through personality" includes the universal need for truth, beauty, goodness, joy, happiness, and love. And he knows that this same deep need is in the hearts of others. Any answer that a preacher offers other people must be in response to a question. A sermon that attempts to answer a question that nobody has asked is the definition of boring.

A spiritual life that includes prayer, reading, serving, and living with those in the community causes the preacher to speak of unavoidable and crucial questions. The preacher must answer some questions that every human on earth will ask: How did life come to be? Is there purpose and design to it all? What is the meaning of life? Why is life worth living?

Does being part of the body of Christ make any difference? What is the key to happiness? What does joy look like?

Meaning and purpose is bound up in those questions. To be a human is to be a question. The answer is not always inside us. People are looking for something more and better. They want to know that ultimate reasonableness of reality that threatens and is so menacing to all.

How does one preach the Word of God to people who have decided to depose their Creator and to put themselves in charge? Under the addictions or sins, people need to hear the Good News more than anything else, yet so many dismiss preaching as futile, fatuous, and insipid. Preaching God's healing Word gives people back their souls.

Herbert Lockyear wrote about 7,457 promises that God has given to humankind. The promise of God's presence is always given with the call to preach so Jesus must be encountered. God tells us to have no fear for God is with us. God's presence makes it possible to accomplish this awesome work. God understands what we are doing and promises to support us.

Speaking a word that challenges people to change, to see and do things differently, creates a sense of isolation that overwhelms the strongest without the Holy Spirit who understands and supports us in our ministry.

God's presence is something we can count on.

More than any other, God realizes the toll preaching takes on us because our Lord knew us thoroughly before we were conceived in the womb and understood, even then, exactly what being a preacher would cost us.

The Joy of Preaching

God promises divine assistance with the actual work. Seasoned preachers know what it is like to open the Bible, to pray, to study, and to listen for what God wants us to preach. Sometimes we feel distressed and we hear nothing. In all our years of preaching at times we preach intently, but we spot a frown, a blank face, a yawn, and a child drawing just as we try to concentrate on our job. On other days, we experience waking up after fervent prayer, with a wonderful fresh idea that fills us with excitement. God, our unseen companion, has been doing more than sightseeing. Our Lord is always there to help us.

There is no greater joy in the preaching life than to discover that embracing the call to preach has placed us in a special relationship with God. His Word brought everything into existence. That Word sustains everything in being by his life-giving presence. And that Word is from One who loves all that he has made, including us, with unconditional love.

Here we are now living on this planet together. Where did we come from? We are not responsible for bringing about ourselves. We did not create ourselves. Our existence is not by our own doing. Most things about ourselves cannot be changed. We ask, "Who made me?" We ask, "Who?" not "what?" God decided to put me in this world. So we are acts of God's mercy. God decided it was good for each one of us to exist. If God likes us, even loves us, then we are not here to be slaves, but to be free. So our existence has a purpose, a meaning, and a mission.

So it is the task of the preacher to deal with more questions: Where are my desires leading me? Are they good? Can we trust our desires? Is there satisfaction for my desires? What is our drama all about?

Desires suggest a joyous plan just for us. Of course, we are limited. Even our limitations have meaning. We cannot make ourselves happy. We have a difficult time conceiving what happiness looks like. Preaching activates the sense of spirituality. It is reenergized in people, not by a choice or a great idea, but through the happening of Jesus the Christ. The preacher awakens this spiritual awareness if the called one is sensitive to the spirit in one's own life. Preachers invite people to a tender and impassioned awareness of themselves that makes them open to the joy of living.

Preaching for the Sake of God's People

The one who preaches cannot help but develop a deep caring for people. The Word of God is born out of love. The Word of God is God's appeal to come to him and let him bring them into eternal life. We must never forget that the reason God called us is to benefit the people.

My close friends and my family know of my life's hills and valleys. God knows the sheer joys that overwhelm me when we are with our spouses and our children. God knows the quickening of spirit that we experience when we are able to speak a word that actually helps someone who is in a difficult situation. And God knows how wonderfully the faint glowing embers of faith are fanned into white hot flames within us through the faithful witness made by the sick and dying when we come to bring them a word of comfort.

Often we struggle with a healing word that needs to be preached. We ache inside to find a story that will make it possible for people to see what this word has to do with them. We wrack our brains and pray ourselves to sleep. And joy comes in that mourning and the image or the story is there.

The flow of the created sermon is so clear that we are mysteriously awestruck. We realize that God has been busy while we were sleeping, giving assistance to our own creativity.

Sometimes we come to preach when we are physically sick. Yet as we speak the Word from God, we are suddenly filled with an energy that we cannot understand. The words flow out as we stand and preach.

People request a copy or tape of our sermons to give to others because the words could help them too. We then discover that the work which we put so much time and effort into really makes a difference for people. God has called us to serve is one of our greatest joys.

Chapter Two
The Joy in the Preparation

PREACHING INVOLVES HARD WORK. It is not possible to practice and prepare for a long time any kind of work if one finds no joy in it, especially if that work must be something of excellence. So where is the joy in this tremendous effort?

Effective preaching requires one to be a wordsmith, a psychologist, a teacher, and a counselor as the called one works language into something beautiful and meaningful. Times of joy is experienced in developing an approach to some aspect of God's word that promises to help the people who receive it.

Times of surprising joy is found in learning to use our voices and our bodies in ways that enhance the meaning of the words we carefully have created.

The Joy of Preaching

Times of self-esteemed joy come as people benefit from our preparation.

Times of anticipated joy come as our words bring that joy into the lives of people we care about so much. If any preacher is open to it, each moment in the preparation for preaching can be a time of joy.

The Experience of a Preacher

I went to a Baptist college to begin my preparation for service to God through the preaching. My view of the preaching task was quite simple. Learning to preach for me was like tying shoes. A person became a good preacher through viewing those who were already good at it. It was similar to shooting free-throws in basketball, watching others and how they do it, enabled one to become a free-throw scorer.

While I realized that future ministers had to learn about the Bible, theology, philosophy, biblical languages, and church history. When it came to preaching, I believed that you either had the gift or you didn't.

Good Southern Baptist preachers went four years to college, then three or four years of seminary, and of course, you had to earn a Ph.D., if you got called to someplace that paid well.

James McReynolds

Did you ever wonder why so many preachers in the past got a doctor of philosophy degree from New College at the University of Edinburgh? One summer I did some continuing education there

I looked at the dissertations found in the library. Most of the works showed no real scholarship as required back then.

My study program leader was with a well-known Scotland preacher named James Stewart. So we can learn from anywhere.

I have experienced many different preachers with various styles. I soon realized you could not copy somebody else, but you developed your own style. At Carson-Newman University (then college) every student was required to attend chapel services. We heard many preachers, fine musicians, and secular speakers. Every student took Bible classes.

The Old Testament prophets became people living real lives, preaching outrageous things, and getting themselves in all kinds of trouble. Every person in every academic major studied Bible.

I attended seminary at Midwestern Baptist Theological Seminary in Kansas City, and five years at Vanderbilt University Divinity School.

In church history classes with Hugh Wamble at Midwestern, I read not only history and biographies, but sermons of preachers. I enjoyed reading the sermons of John Wesley. Connecting to the

The Joy of Preaching

larger historic community of preachers has inspired me for many years. I took history of preaching and many preaching, worship, and literature courses under John Killinger and the excellent faculty at Vanderbilt. I learned more about American history with a course on "Preaching in American History" by Herman Norton, a Disciples of Christ minister and professor.

The church benefits from a minister who has experienced the formal study in a theological seminary or a divinity school.

Ministry is strengthened when in a formal manner a pastor is exposed to biblical studies, biblical languages, church history, theology, practical studies, pastoral care, and philosophy, as well as preaching. Such ministers usually have better capacity for vision and doing ministry in a local church. Nothing substitutes for service within a body of Christ with its multitudes of daily challenges.

Now I have been preaching for 60 years. I have served every type of congregation from First Baptist Church in Knoxville as a student minister to planting new churches. My preaching has made a difference to many people. Keeping this in mind has been enough to chase away the clouds of discouragement and allow me to find joy in the ministry of preaching once again.

Making connections with preachers of the past has been a lifeline over the years. At times the darkness of living has been so thick I could not see the fire of faith or the light of truth glowing. Joy seldom came as I felt badly about preaching while I was so out of touch with God myself.

Many preachers have inspired me, but my favorite is Jesus. He spoke in the language of the people. John Killinger, Fred Craddock, Frederick Buechner, and Barbara Taylor give me joy in being part of this great company of witnesses.

While serving the church at the Sunday School Board, I taught preaching at the American Baptist Theological Seminary in Nashville. I took a course on "Black Preaching" at Vanderbilt and I was humbly honored to hear excellent preaching from my young African American students. Every preacher needs to experience their tradition. That's the joy of preaching.

Chapter 3
Encountering Jesus in the Word of God

PREACHING EXISTS IN THE CHURCH AS an encounter with the living Word of God which Saint John says is Jesus.

How many people to whom we preach are struggling with illness, addictions, relationships, jobs, or other issues in living life?

The presence of Christ by way of the presence of the preacher can help people to become themselves. People need His Presence to free them from the decay.

Irrevocable joy can be the response whenever the Bible is read and interpreted in the assembly of God's people. The ongoing experience of such joy is the greatest blessing of the preaching life. Preachers spend many hours dwelling with the Word of God to identify the riches it holds. So we are blessed.

The method of dwelling with the Word has been called lectio divina. It works as the preacher begins by reading a text from the Bible. The scripture is read slowly until a word or a phrase grabs the attention of the reader. At that time the preacher stops reading and reflects on that word or phrase. Secluded in one's study or in a covenant group, the preacher receives a word from God, a gift of understanding that guides the spiritual journey to the heart of the kingdom. So the Word is embraced. Prayer is the next step as one receives the blessing of being equipped to create a life-giving message.

When the Spirit gives a text, it is not just for the preacher. It is a word of life to the entire faith community. The Bible is read as a source for the sermon. For years I allowed a 12 year old to read the text. The message flows from the reading of the Bible. Sometimes I have the congregation stand in reverence for the Word of God and the mysteries of faith which we will receive after the reading of the source for the encounter with Jesus the Christ.

Most mainline preachers use the lectionary for sermon texts. The lectionary is a three cycle of texts that most preachers find useful and much help from the internet. Also, there they find sermons on the weekly lectionary text. The lectionary assures that the church and the pastor will cover needed Bible material and not favored texts as the only topics. Some preachers have an agenda. Some may preach on the woes of a political party in power. Every text goes back to some secular theme. God expects growth.

Charles Spurgeon died in his 50's. He served in a golden age of preaching. Each Sunday, he preached to as many as 5,000. One good book on preaching is his Lectures to My Students. I also have his volumes of sermons.

In that book, he wrote, "I would sooner bring one sinner to Jesus Christ than unravel all the mysteries of the divine Word, because salvation is the one thing we are to live for."

In many of my pastorates, I have used the lectionary. Music, prayers, and traditional creeds are prepared a year in advance in the congregation. Preaching then is on one theme or text.

So the preacher fits her words into the religious ritual. Some churches limit the sermon to eight to ten minutes.

But what if the lectionary texts for a week are not pertinent for the community need. What about the times when there are deaths or a tragic killing of children? What if the given text is awkward for the preaching event that Sunday?

Some churches resist having the theology or guidance of an outside authority. In the movie Chocolate, the lay leader in the church has to approve what the preacher is to say. He was the mayor of the town and enjoyed the power he had over the body of Christ. In the end he loosened up and the congregation came alive. The preacher preached with joy on his face. Even the traditional mayor came alive and experienced joy.

In my opinion the Good News of preaching can never be forced. Peter preached what the Holy Spirit led him. Preaching God's Word can only be received by its ability to convict, encounter, and convert the hearts of free thinkers. If sermons are based upon everyone accepting the Word of God, the ministry and vision for the church will not go far.

Much of my preaching today is a series of messages shared from a Bible book, a timely topic, or a theological confusion about living the Christian life.

People may bring their Bibles. Sometimes the outline is in the bulletin or on a worship screen.

Because we preach for a particular community it is helpful to receive direct input from the members of that community.

Some preachers enjoy being a member of a support group for sharing insights on the biblical material. Talking it over with the church's leaders helps to clarify the connections between the biblical text and the congregation.

The Joy of Preaching

Receiving Jesus' life inside is the encounter.

Worship is the event in people's lives which we encounter the living Christ. Taking Jesus as personal savior, letting Jesus in, throwing light on life, gaining proper balance, being saved, and being in the Presence are phrases that describe this encounter.

Christianity is not just an idea or an ethical choice, but a Person.

This encounter is God's method of salvation. Prayer, study, and weekly assembly in the body of Christ are essential as we are being saved every day of our lives. The presence of Jesus can take place and becomes normative for our lives.

At times, sometimes after more than 50 years of preparing sermons, sparks will be flying, light bulbs popping, and knowing and feeling Jesus, messages will come in powerful rushes. In times of deep and intimate praying, suddenly any clouds of darkness will go away, and we are touched again with the joy of preaching.

Dwelling with the Word results in many fresh insights into the life of faith. One cannot share all the insights and we must avoid any temptation because most preaching has some time limitation.

Joyous worship involves so much more than the message.

James McReynolds

During most of my pastorates, I have the outline of the sermon in the bulletin and on the worship screen. Good preaching needs a focus and a main point. Is there a specific word needed by the church at this particular time?

One sermon will not transform a congregation. Years of preaching over time, will shape the church's outreach and reputation. During college and seminary, young preachers give energy to learn biblical interpretation theology and prepare sermons.

When one finally completes the seminary training and receives a call or is appointed by a superior authority to a particular church, the focus of ministry may have to change.

Our vision for the church the past few years is "to create an atmosphere where joy and miracles happen." Joy is the hook that gives every message a specific purpose. It is such a joy to know that, by the Lord's grace, we have something precious and vital to share with those we love.

Before we begin any creation, we must pray. We must ask the Holy Spirit to enable us to discern the word that God would have us preach. Pray with your church directory or photos of the people as you seek to stay aware of their problems or joys with images of those whom I am their minister. We must be mindful of the baggage we have with us as we encounter these precious souls.

The Joy of Preaching

God speaks to us in multitudes of ways as we dwell with the Word. We are changed as our church changes. Those days when the juices are not flowing and the joy is not there, prayer gives us a stimulus for spiritual growth. This drives us to keep on our life-long study of the Bible.

The joy of responding to Jesus makes us want to stay with our Lord, to live a relationship with him, to embrace what is important to God and to make it our own. Preaching does that. The possibility of becoming a Christian depends on the encounter with Jesus who gives life a new horizon.

To approach preaching in any other way amounts to reducing the communication of his Word to some kind of abstraction. No matter how "sound" is our theology or how brilliant our insights, it misses the point.

Only by an encounter do people turn around and become Christians. It is all about Jesus, not a message. Preaching is not to just make a speech. It is never a discourse. It is a happening involving a person called by God and that is a mystery.

We continue to capture and re-capture the joys of preaching when we prayerfully return to what has happened to us personally.

Each sermon is about what happened in an event. The event is new, exciting, provoking surprise and wonder. We find something new that keeps on creating something new. It takes hold of us and impinges upon our daily lives in every conceivable way to keep us faithful.

People look to the preacher to see Jesus' Presence from which the called one draws his own strength. Preaching takes the form of an encounter because the possibility of being Christian is the result of an encounter with Jesus the Christ.

What is attractive to the one called to preach about the encounter with the living Jesus is just what is attractive to others. The perception that the preacher and others in the body of Christ have "something different" in their living is what makes all the difference for the hearers of the preaching. That creative newness is the joy of preaching.

Chapter 4
The Cross of Giving Something Good Every Time

THE CALLED PREACHER IS EXPECTED TO create something good every time. The short time devoted to reading the Bible passage and the sermon after the long process of praying, reading the Bible, study, meditation, writing, and editing staggers our imagination..

No matter how many hours one spends to do something good, the Word is God's to impart. The preacher's communication skills are the one thing that connects a congregation to receive the intended message. Telling jokes or stories with no connection with the Word will send people home with thoughts that cause them to never return.

James McReynolds

Preaching is serious business. Some sermons are intensive, others are extensive. Some follow clear outlines. These are logical and the outline enables memory and understanding about the particular day's preaching event.

With the gift of being evocative, a sermon may suggest images and impressions which linger in the heart and mind long after the worship ends. These images become triggers for the local church's vision and mission.

Our most effective sermons are deceptively simple. Simplicity is not the same as simplistic. Simplistic is a statement of the obvious. Nothing is worse than having the listening congregation respond to the sermon by thinking, "So what?"

Simple is like a persuasive testimony by an eyewitness in a murder trial. Simple is an announcement of the president in the face of a crisis. Simple truths pierce to the heart. Listeners learn that things could be different. Life could be full of joy.

God called me to be a communicator. Preaching, teaching, writing, and counseling are all necessary in the pastor's life.

After Carson-Newman where my major was English, I knew I was a writer, and I had no desire to get a doctorate in English. So I attended the University of Missouri-Columbia School of

Journalism. The base of a journalism class is to learn the five "W's." Good articles in magazines and newspapers require answers to who, what, where, when, and why. These are the questions people expect from books, newsletters, and sermons.

Technical language from theological or biblical interpretation causes most of the congregation to think the sermon was from some beyond that is beyond them. People need and desire to hear from the Word of God or no encounter will take place.

Most sermons are saturated with religious language, calls to grow spiritually, and reassurances that God loves us. Most contain a lot of God talk, but precious little good news.

Those sermons are overloaded with references to God. What they mean by God is a projection of religious sentiment which has been in the community church eons ago. So the sermon is not new nor news. Nothing exciting or newsworthy is found. It does allude to the Bible, refers to God, and gives some wise advice.

But people ask, "What is happening here today?" We can put our sermons to a test: does this message tells us that God in Jesus Christ will come to encounter us and for us to be brought to the Lord through the Word of God. Is the sermon helping us to see what God is doing even now inside our beings and our souls? Does our preaching really offer news?

James McReynolds

Preachers receiving a call from God are in an awesome work. The responsibility is to share God's Word in a way that will help people to receive it. We must be creative. We have to summon all the skills both natural and acquired to fashion something that will cause others to receive Jesus' encountering word.

Creating "something good," involves paying attention to questions that are asked. They are almost always meant for us.

A sermon is not on the Bible passages, but a message from and through them. What is implied but not explicitly stated? What is read between the lines? Be sensitive as a novelist and pay close attention to "clues" the author has included to get to the heart of the mysterious story.

How does this passage relate to the entire scriptures? Observe the context of the passage within the whole biblical writing. What comes before and after the writing? Are there accounts of the same event in the other gospels or other books of the Bible? Some details give insight that is not insignificant or coincidental. What does the biblical writing reveal about Jesus?

Prayerfully reflect on all you have considered. Let us reflect on the story of the woman at the well in the gospel of John. Look at the word "thirst." What does John mean by thirst? Is there any relation to Jesus' word from the cross when he said, "I thirst?"

What insight do we get from the woman's question? What is the "spring of water welling up to eternal life? How is this woman feeling in response to Jesus? What is a prophet? Where else does this dramatic form appear in John's gospel? Why does the woman leave her water jar behind? Why would the people believe a person that was considered worthless and why did they go out to meet Jesus?

Answering these and other similar questions help the preacher create something good. The divine word is fully revealed as the Bible is read again and again. So much can be achieved by digging into the Word even before consulting a commentary.

A really good sermon enables one's hearers to encounter any familiar passage in a new way. "Something good" can be created every time we preach if we let God give you insight and passion.

Use the entire scriptures in the Bible to let God challenge us. In some older congregations, grief is real. Grief may even be the "elephant" in the sanctuary. Those in grief need to learn how to be joyful and even to laugh again. Some of us use a weekly newsletter to set the stage for the preached word. Some discussion can be best done through the printed page. When some ideas, dreams, and visions are first shared in a pastoral reflection and then followed by a thought producing sermon, the effectiveness is increased and the pastoral reflection becomes firmly grounded in biblical faith.

James McReynolds

God works in the soul of the preacher in mysterious ways. God honors us by enabling us to use our abilities in ways that will help in the accomplishment of his work.

Before God can speak through one's personality, we must be surrendered to the spirit's leading and opening the souls of his children. Over the years in ministry, many tools are mastered.

Experience and awareness of one's skills come from observation, practice, and a desire to create something good and beautiful and serviceable.

Using our unique gifts, graces, and style in the act of preaching is important as it underscores the variety of personalities and abilities of each minister. People will come to hear you. They'll talk about just how you are different. Also, they can tell how they are different.

Ministers do honor when possible local worship traditions, but they should not be forced to give up the sling shot in favor of armor of Saul. For example, a pastor might refuse to use film clips as a tool if that does not mesh with one's style of preaching. Some would rather dress in a polo shirt and slacks than wear a robe and a stole.

Positive responses in the congregation are not the result of one's skills. In a growing suburb or new community where there are no other local churches, people might join in multitudes even with poor but honest preaching. A church near a military base or in a university town might have 500 additions each year (and many requests for their letters) as the norm. Preachers are never the focus in the church. The congregation can go on fulfilling its vision despite who the pastor might be. Preachers or pastors come and go but the people in the church remain. That's why humility is the most valuable character trait for any preacher.

No minister of Word and sacrament can be excused for the sloppiness and casual laziness that gives the impression that what is being done really isn't that important.

Preachers do many important things as a minister, but preaching is the most important. Pastoral care is needed. So is administration, teaching, and sharing in the denominational work, but only by preaching do we help people with vital issues such as anger and despair, pain and forgiveness, grief and going on with life, conflict and transformation.

Ministers lose confidence in the importance of preaching. Televisions blare all day and all night. People can't relate to just verbal communication. They want communication to involve all our senses. My doctor of ministry dissertation at Vanderbilt Divinity School was titled, "Sensitivity Group Insights and the Preaching Ministry of the Church." The title dates my work completed back in 1972. It included preaching in the electronic environment with McLuhan influence, dialogically-oriented preaching, and the implications of small groups in the church. Taste, touch, silence, sound, awareness, multi-media, imagination, and the exposure of the weaknesses in our preaching in changing times and changing media.

Monologue preaching and the use of personal monologues as when a minister with theatrical skills assumes the character of such people as Ruth, Mary, Miriam, Hannah, Esther, Mary Magdalene,

Lydia, and the unnamed women. Also, there are the words and times of Jesus, Paul, Peter, Moses, or Abraham.

Some ministers are exceedingly effective, convincing actors and thus, the congregation encounters the message from the character's dress, the words, body movement, and perhaps even the background scenery.

No minister of God worthy of the title ever neglects the finer demands of preparing "something good" requiring hard work, creativity and skillful presentation. Preachers must be spirit filled as this important work is not done in a vacuum. The enemies of Christ and his church are excellent communicators. They persuade people to hold on to their own pleasures and sins that are contrary to the Good News of the gospel.

Because of this reality, preachers must do everything possible to become excellent communicators themselves. The goal is to have

The Joy of Preaching

a word to share with people. It has been helpful for me to be able to write down the focus of the sermon in a single sentence.

Many of the members of our congregations are intelligent, seeking guidance, and not patient to hear one ramble or yell at them.

Those kind of messages end with wasting of the congregation's time, and they will leave without anything to hang on to as they struggle in their spiritual and human lives.

Something good happens in an honest, skillful sharing of the Word of God. Good preaching causes people to rejoice in the good things God is doing for them. The encounter helps them learn something new. It helps them to see how they have strayed from following Christ. And they step one step further in their walk with the Christ.

The best older book on preaching for me was *For We Have This Treasure* written by Paul E. Scherer as the Yale Lectures on

Preaching for 1943. Scherer was one of John Killinger's professors. This classic book focuses on the theme, "If you ever want to set anybody on fire, you have to burn a little yourself."

A more recent classic is Fred Craddock's book *Preaching*.

James McReynolds
Let your creative juices flow.

What do you do when the joy of preaching becomes the drudgery of preaching? Constant creativity is a must for the preaching ministry. To get back our enthusiasm, we must pray to renew the relationship we have with God who called us.

Simply begin by brainstorming by jotting down anything that comes to mind that appears to be related to our purpose.

Perhaps you will remember a news article, television program, or a movie or a bumper sticker, a painting, a comic strip, or a song on the radio. Get relaxed. Remember your call. Listen to some of your past sermons. Confidence will come back. It is amazing and mysterious what kind of resources will be gathered.

Write down your thoughts and stimulations or you will forget them.

****

The beginning of your message must engage your congregation. Do not use too many illustrations or examples or long quotes.

Avoid using material that might be good, but does not fit the purpose of the message. Never use material that does not connect with the life experience of the people. Never use the contents of a pastoral counseling session. Personal stories can demonstrate the preacher's understanding of the lives and struggles. They create a greater openness to receiving the message. Keep personal stuff to a minimum. Credit for materials from another source should be acknowledged. Preaching is different from reading, as it is oral communication.

Preachers must be able to write well. Honing my writing skills through my University of Missouri School of Journalism degree has proven to be a great asset in preparation of sermons.

Something good might not happen because the one who wrote it did not prepare to preach it. The preaching encounter is not done on paper. It is oral and visual. Speech classes can give principles of oral communication. Most oral communications are sophisticated and polished, so why should preaching not be as good in clarity in inflection, pitch, volume, and rate of speaking.

Times of experiencing sheer joy can be found in working language into something good, meaningful, and beautiful. Joy is found in fulfillment of the anticipation of helping to bring joy into the lives of people we love. Jesus challenged his hearers to a conversion of life that means setting aside things that keeps people from embracing Jesus.

Creating something that is acceptable in the body of Christ need not require compromise. Every intelligent high school student realizes that the view of life by the biblical writers had been proven obsolete by science and modern physics. Preachers must not blink at this reality nor should they resist it. A group of students from the science classes of a public school went to the museum at the University of Nebraska that features skeletal bones and large pictures of the world a million years ago. One teacher who goes to a so-called fundamentalist church said that it was all made up because her Schofield Bible clearly says God created the world in seven literal days only about 4,000 years ago. When a preacher dares to share the teachings of Jesus, she fears sharing the cross of preaching found in some obstinate people. The Bible is not a science book, a book of religious rules, or traditions. It is a spiritual Word for people living today. Some say preaching is not what it used to be. Ministers could preach in public schools without having the event held outside the school buildings.

In some of my early pastorates, the worship was aired on the radio . . . free of charge. Preaching really mattered. People came on Sunday morning and night and again on Wednesday night. Churches then and now want the district superintendent to appoint somebody who knows how to preach. It is also true in most any denominated or independent congregation. They call for a good preacher. The cross of trying to defend a lost past rather than do a dangerous march into the future.

Preaching something good is inhibited by the lectionary which covers only a portion of the Bible. How does the church justify a system that excludes so much of our Bibles?

The Joy of Preaching

I find that most congregations enjoy series preaching. The lectionary is designed for congregations to view the entire Bible.

The aim of preaching must be relevance. Life is hard. We need to preach on difficult texts. From the troubling passages from the Bible come sermons that make a difference in life's chaos.

Every preacher wants to be effective and interesting. We want to preach the Word of God in a way that the people will remember. They file thousands of possible illustrations to gain for fresh insights. Preachers do want to be unique in style do that they can allow God to speak through them. They must build on the elements of their own personality. There is a special child of God inside every preacher, and no two are the same.

Connecting to the culture of a particular church and the particular people in this particular church is so difficult that some ministers want to quit within a year. Ministers are guided into being better informed about the Bible than about the culture of the mission field to which they are called to serve.

Longer pastorates are needed for pastors to observe how much they really need to learn. A lifetime of academic training can create a minister's status group with their own spirituality, vocabulary, values, and expectations which widens the gap between the pastor and his people. In some places, it may take ten years to be a part of a church's family. Pastors come and go, but the people stay.

So pastors must focus on connecting in the early years. Ministers come to learn what the people will accept. They also learn what the community needs. They ask about the emphasis God wants this particular community of faith to hear at this particular time in history. The preacher can help the church to see where we have been and where God can lead us in our future together. Nobody can create a new past for the church. It's gone no matter how much we talk about it.

No pastorate is easy. A preacher can be crucified in most any kind of congregation. There is such a cross that sometimes "something good" every time is ammunition for the preacher killers to do just that. Still the local church with all our hypocrites and self-serving leaders, is where it is in preaching. Any congregation can make you a better preacher. All of us has had good and bad matches as we serve as ministers of word and sacrament.

The cross of an unhealthy congregation or a bitter, mean supervisor can destroy preachers and their family members. Divorce is rampant with ministers. The cross of presenting something good every time we preach can create low self-esteem, depression, and loneliness among those called to preach the joy of the Lord.

The Joy of Preaching

I have loved every single body of Christ in which I have shared my experience with Jesus. I once served a church that had the world's smallest cross on top, about six inches tall.

I enjoy all kinds of church music. Music wars between so-called contemporary and traditional are a tool of the devil. Some of my churches could not afford an instrumentalist who could play the modern forms of hymns. So young people who encountered Jesus through preaching the Word of God in any of the bodies of Christ I have served would accept any musical expression of the faith. We can all profit from the Serenity Prayer: "Lord give me the serenity to accept the things I cannot change, the courage to change the things I can, and the wisdom to know the difference."

Contemporary Christian singer Twyla Paris shares the beauty of every congregation in her words: "How beautiful the hands that served the wine and the bread and the sons of the earth. How beautiful the feet that walked the long dusty roads and the hills to the cross. How beautiful, how beautiful is the body of Christ."

Paris goes on in her song to sing: "How beautiful the radiant Bride who waits for her Groom with His light in her eyes. How beautiful when humble hearts give the fruit of pure lives so that others may live. How beautiful . . . is the body of Christ. How beautiful the feet that bring the sound of good news and the love of the King.

How beautiful the hands that serve the wine and the bread and the sons of the earth. How beautiful . . . is the body of Christ."

Being just good enough is not what we want when a director of missions, district superintendent, executive presbyter, regional minister, or bishop shows up to visit your church and to hear you preach.

If we do not have any misgivings about our sermon, we might have some now. With a busy week of sickness in our family, funerals, and more and more meetings, we might have not fine-tuned the message. So we moan, "Why didn't she decide to visit us three weeks ago when I had a good sermon, all polished well, and ten people made professions of faith in Jesus?"

Why should we worry about our efforts to be good every time we speak? Some great teacher once said, "Great sermons are great obstacles for the Holy Spirit." Who are we seeking to please? The congregation does not need a polished and well-crafted message.

They need something prepared with much prayer with a word specifically for their congregation. Being their pastor, all of us know our audience as other speakers cannot. This close relationship is reflected in what we say.

Some sermons go well in one church, but not so good in another church where one does not know the people. Effective preaching has a personal effort. People will respond to the Word of God if we have ministered to them personally. If we go out of our way to visit or make a phone call to someone in a crisis, they get more out of my efforts. If our pastoral care has disappointed them, their ears close even to my best sermons.

Most preachers suffer from perfection disorders. We are just too proud to be only "good enough preachers." If a church loves us, they will go along so far with poor or mediocre sermons. Do your best despite the limitations. As much as 90 per cent of pastors also have another job. Bi-vocational pastors or poorly paid ones as numerous in small congregations located in remote places. God expects his ministers to do the best we can even with limitations. We must expect the time and schedule that we have in a given week.

When our time is tight, we might be tempted to forego our study time and be dishonest with the chosen text from God's Word. Reading the Holy Scripture is a precious moment. Sometimes the congregation stands as the Bible is read. The congregation expects the sermon to depend on the message in the scripture text, but some use any biblical text as a springboard to whatever thoughts or personal bias they may have such as a political agenda, some specific topic that everybody agrees with. That kind of preaching is not "good enough" anytime.

James McReynolds

Confidence comes to us as west rest in the calling God has given to us. Preaching God's Word is serious business, most demanding, yet we can enjoy it. That's the joy of preaching.

Chapter 5
Putting the Word of God into Human Words

PERHAPS YOU HAVE SEEN A SERMON that used no words, only pictures, candles, a cross, or the still small voice of silence. However, most of the time we expect a sermon with sound. Sound places us in the middle of an encounter. Music immerses us into a world that we choose to enter. People enjoy "surround sound" because of the semblance of presence. Sound gives us an existential experience. Sound gives an atmosphere of mystery. Sound means that there is someone or something present. Sound demands our attention, our wonder, our concern. What we see is not as powerful as what we hear. That has implications for preaching the Word.

The number one fear is public speaking. Not even death is more fearful. Sound reveals what is interior about a person or a thing. If we speak out loud in front of others, we expose our interior self. We stand before others spiritually naked.

We cannot conceive a voice apart from the person to whom it belongs. Even the voice of a dead person recorded on tape envelops us with this presence as no picture can. Jesus told us that the voice of the shepherd leads and guides his sheep. The Shepherd's voice indicates presence.

When the Word became flesh, God did not sent an inscribed Word. The Word was spoken. The preaching ministry continues this event of the incarnation.

Jesus preached in a mode that reached his audience. This is the genius of using parables.

The encounter with Jesus that preaching brings about begins with the preacher's voice. The power of voice causes the hearer to be aware of a presence, to reach into the interior of people as to speak to his deepest self, and to generate presence and mystery. Preaching then prompts people to follow Jesus.

Communication has consequences. A thoughtless word hurts us deep in our beings. The lives of people who enjoy happiness depends on the communication they respond to every day.

The Joy of Preaching

It is the preacher's responsibility to find fresh and compelling language capable of breaking through the spiritual blindness and deafness that imprison so many people.

We contrast what we want to preach with the Bible's clearly stated aim and purpose. What we preach may not be our personal idea, but we ate bound to the Word of God. We want our people to hear what Jesus can give them and to get the congregation to respond to that word.

People hear Jesus speaking through the speech of our preaching. Sharing God's Word through the word of the preacher can be a healing for those who respond to it.

In preaching the funeral sermon for Irene Bond, the 94 year old matriarch of our church, the congregation was enjoying themselves. Funny stories were told about her faithful life. The church was filled.

One family expressed it well: "That's the first time I found joy at a funeral." The preacher always delights in speaking of those who are loved. Some of the times we know joy in life is that personal memory of those we love.

When standing to preach, the people gathered together want us to speak of what we love. We take the words of everyday life and use them to speak for God.

James McReynolds

People always say, the pastor "preached his/her funeral." Preaching gets a privileged place. Nothing in life affects people more than the death of a loved one. The beloved family closest to the one who has died are still moving about in a fog. They are disoriented, present from what is going on.

Ministers who love people can't help but be profoundly affected themselves. As they come before people to speak of God, they bring their own wounds inflicted by past experiences with death. They use words to bring healing words of life. Of all settings for preaching, the funeral often has the most total in attendance.

The funeral sermon cries out the most for the sharing of a word that will enable God's people to continue on their journey toward the kingdom of God. The funeral brings a unique opportunity and a special challenge. The audience is made up of people who are not regular church goers. The focus is spiritual as is expected. Death brings people into the church to hear the words of faith.

Preaching at a funeral requires sensitivity to those who will attend the life celebration. We do not want to focus too much on the sadness of the situation that we make it impossible for people to experience the moments of joy and the consolation of Christian faith. We are there to cause people to think that their own faith is inadequate by ignoring their loss. Preachers must be sensitive to the truth. We must not portray a notorious and mean sinner as a saint. We must be compassionately honest.

A word from the Word of God enables people to receive a word that will help them face the prospects and certainty of their own deaths. As those who grieve are helped to embrace their creator God during such a difficult time, there is no greater joy.

Wedding words from the context of a production where a couple transgresses modesty or moderation pushes the preacher to the limit. Sometimes the couple has a disregard for the church and they never attend except for funerals and weddings distract the preacher and they can feel the energy draining out. This is not the case of all weddings. Some weddings are a privileged moment for preaching.

No matter what the motivation, people have come for their wedding in a church, so church is what they will get. We want to present them the church at its best. The preacher wants the words to show how committed love gives life to a couple, to their friends and families, and to the world. Most wedding assemblies are a tough crowd to reach. If preaching the Word is requested, the sermon helps keep the couple focused. So it is a privilege to see on the faces of the congregation gathered signs that the word I have been given by God to proclaim is reaching deep into their souls. This is why we preach to encounter Jesus at a wedding, a place where Jesus performed his first miracle.

There is no end to the places where preachers share a sermon: hospital chapels, prisons and jails, schools, parks, care centers, youth groups, rallies, celebrations, homeless living places, saloons, truck stops, under trees, brush arbors, or anywhere people will gather.

Doing the thing you love to do might cause some to work too long and too hard and actually do too much preaching.

If we are to be faithful preachers, we must be faithful human beings. We need to go deeper with Jesus leading us to a happy life despite our cross of preaching. If one wants to serve the ministry of preaching the Word of God for 50 or more years, you had best get a life. Constant preaching or praying enlivens you or wears you down.

If you are suffering from preaching burnout, you might look at your approach or your speaking schedule. We do not have to be in a hurry, but we must obey and allow the spirit to live in us. A preacher's date book reveals their health.

Some ministers never get to eat out, buy new clothes, purchase a home, buy a new car, or enjoy the simple pleasures of life. Too much time reading the Word, preaching, and serving a flock can bring numbing, dead feeling when the call of the Lord becomes a horrid, depressing chore. Do something that to you has always been fun to refresh your soul.

Ever since fourth grade, I have enjoyed playing basketball. A few years back, I joined a fitness club. It was about 30 miles from my home. My wife Laurel joined me. We worked out, ran, and went through a series of exercises with nice equipment. I think heaven might have a basketball gym for me. I started shooting free throws, but could hardly reach the basket from 15 feet. I practiced daily. Soon I was swishing the nets. I got better than ever at age 65. I played in pick-up games with much younger people. Soon I could keep up with the others. I began to hit 20 to 30 to 40 consecutive free throws. One night I actually made 77 free throws in a row.

Even three pointers became regular. I could hit three pointers from all around the three point circle. That sure helped an old man's esteem.

But then gasoline prices began to soar. The monthly fees were too pricey. So we decided that we needed to quit. I never got back into shape and have not shot a basketball since.

Ministers must appreciate the many gifts God gives for us to enjoy in this world. We could do many things for our health such as playing catch with a child, yoga, gardening, hiking, playing guitar, tennis, softball, ice cream, painting in oils, quilting, throwing horseshoes, or going on a date with your wife.

To really enjoy life seems foreign to those who have no clue. People think the preacher should suffer for humanity, so some preachers believe that to be called to preach the Word of God is to live a miserable life. They just give and give until there is nothing to give. Suffering with other Christians whom we serve is different from suffering to replace their suffering with yours. Do the members of your congregation experience joys in life? Are they happy? Are we as a congregation a bunch of people who love misery or chaos in living? No wonder the world with all its pleasure seeking do not see the church as a place to share the happiness of the kingdom of God.

Fickle congregations tempt preachers to pander to their political or cultural mindset. So they avoid the controversial, even if the message is from the Bible. They try to make people smile with jokes or stating how they are right and others are wrong. A preacher at Ridgecrest Conference Center in North Carolina once was judged by some ministers. One man said, after hearing the sermon, "I think he said something liberal." Another replied, "Well what did he say?" He answered, "I don't know, but it sure sounded liberal to me." In our day some might say, "I think she said something that appeared too conservative . . . ." Let the Word be the Word.

Some enjoy the limelight of addressing their assembly or convention. So they design their sermon so the crowd will be excited and in harmony by the end. Un-regenerated preachers and their congregations don't really care about the Word of God.

The Joy of Preaching

They come to the church to be entertained, to feel good about their status in the community. These gatherings with their congregations simple keep a tradition alive. I'm amazed at what happens when the many people go to worship. Some strive to stay the same until they find themselves almost dead with lack of genuine spirituality.

People need and deep inside want a body of Christ created by the Word of God. They will not tolerate the excess baggage that comes with a church tradition that sucks the joy out of life both inside and outside the church.

If you ask what most people remember in our sermons, it is the stories. Stories complement the teaching of the Bible by fleshing out the truth. Stories change lives.

Not far from where I was born in East Tennessee, there is a small town called Jonesborough. More than 12,000 people travel from all around the globe to attend the National storytelling Festival.

The story telling captivates listeners. The audiences sit spellbound for hours listening to the storytellers' unique tales. Stories are sad, joyful, funny, sentimental, fictitious, historical, mythological, hillbilly, and comical. With each diverse story, one feature was in common with everyone. These stories held the power to keep the attention of the hearers.

Storytellers involved the audience by asking listeners to clap, sing, repeat phrases, or do a kind of sign language. Humor was interjected even in the sad stories. They used no notes. Stories are shared as an oral event. Nobody read a story. Each speaker told their story. Audiences were filled with enthusiasm. The smiles on their faces revealed that the storytellers enjoyed what they were doing.

When our minister gets renewed, the preaching also gets renewed. And best of all, the congregation gets renewed. And through sharing the Word of God, transformed people can receive Jesus the source of our joy and strength to live a wonderful life.

We need to be reminded that Jesus said that we must come to the Lord as a child. If the concept of the preacher having fun seems childish, you and your congregation will get over it.

We live in a sound-bite culture with clipped phrases and visual images with people today who have short attention spans. We must be intentional in preaching with use of short sentences, repetition, and visual images.

Biblically centered sermons must be short, sweet, pointed, and poignant. The Good News is that we are not dealing with a distant deity who expects us to climb a religious ladder to qualify for God's favor.

The Joy of Preaching

As preachers, we must be aware that any one of our sermons may be all someone ever knows of us. And even more frightening, it may be all anyone ever knows of the gospel.

The human words we use in speaking the Word of God give our congregations a clear idea of our personalities and passions. We are that transparent.

Our words emanate from sincere, disciplined study. New preachers note this: Great preachers are not born, they are made from years and years of devoted study. Sermons that people will listen to are dividends paid on the preacher's investment of relentless hard work. The congregants are the beneficiaries. And that's the joy of preaching.

Chapter 6
Preaching for People Who Want to Go Back to Egypt

No matter how many times one tells a congregation that salvation is a free gift, some want to pay for it by their works. Being a Christian is not just an ethical choice. It is not being born into a moral family. Some preachers forget preaching is a unique encounter with Jesus Christ. Moral and immoral people then respond to the challenge to the powerlessness found in trying to let Jesus in so that they may live with "the joy of the Lord as their strength."

Doing works or being moral or heeding all the rules, the laws, the dogmas, the commandments of the Christian faith, and some local community "no's" such as no dancing, no drinking, no card playing, no television, no sex, or no anger or war will not give you a ticket to heaven.

Being a Christian is not about what we do. Being a Christian is more about who we are. Becoming a Christian is about an encounter with a person, with Jesus the Christ. Having morals is not saving faith because it can only lead to mere behavior and not to a Person.

Millions try to be moral, but that kind of attempt remains a legalistic way of approaching morality because it reduces religion to ethics or an ideology. Some well-meaning preachers speak of life as a keeping of God's laws instead of a personal friendship with our Higher Power.

So church members cater to the way of original sin by attempts to manage and measure reality according to standards that they can comprehend and control. They reduce the mystery of faith to a list of do's and don'ts. Life is a big problem to be solved, rather than a joyous mystery to be lived.

Such false preaching cause people to think that God desires our moral irreproachability than he is in our union with him in Jesus the Christ. They want to go back to Egypt, to ancient or modern tradition, which was the basis of Jesus' complaints against the scribes and Pharisees.

That kind of preaching places more burdens on people without specifying how the good proposed corresponds to their basic experience which is the needs of their heart and soul. That kind of preaching comes across as unreasonable. Grace is not even part of that equation. People hear what they thought was an encounter with Jesus, but in fact leads them to unhappy lives that substitute pleasures of the world for the joys of the Lord.

In chapter two of Acts, Saint Peter's excellent sermon is recorded. Peter reminds his audience of what happened with Jesus the Christ. So they encountered the meaning of Jesus' death and resurrection so that the people can use their free will to make a judgment about Jesus.

Because Peter's sermon was a compelling encounter, many in that congregation are "cut to the heart." They are now "under conviction" as they hear the message. They then ask Peter, "What shall we do?" They trusted the preacher for guidance and insight into their daily living.

No person has ever been converted to Jesus by hearing truths about Jesus, but having Jesus himself. Jesus talked with the rich young ruler who had an excellent record of commandment keeping. Jesus requires of him a challenge that has never crossed his mind. Jesus asks this young man to sell everything or just give it all away.

Jesus asks him and us to "follow me." The pathetic fact is that like many others have done, he leaves Jesus. He is more attached to his success at keeping the moral laws than he is in having a relationship to the Word of God made flesh and the possibilities for Kingdom life offered in accepting the radical ways of Jesus.

Jesus is never impressed by moral blamelessness but by honest openness. Trying to be above others and holding on to traditions only reinforces the personal hell unbelievers have created for themselves. Many congregations continue to listen to false preaching that gives them nothing but guilt-inducing slavery and not freedom-giving obedience. Obedience to the person Jesus is how we overcome our false selves. We must let Someone in.

Our spiritual sense tell us that the meaning of our lives lies outside us, but in the Mystery who created us. To be fully human, we must look beyond ourselves to our relationship with God. Jesus' own preaching begins with his words in this order:

> "The time is fulfilled and the kingdom of God is at hand repent, and believe in the gospel." (Mark 1:15)

Jesus who is within us makes us want to repent. Our repentance is made possible because we are "in Christ" and Christ is in us. Good preaching is always accomplished by the preacher's personal encounter with the living Christ. Some preachers tell an alcoholic that she must stop drinking because it is bad for his health. Those words are not from the Word, because every person who depends on alcohol gets sick, vomits all day, experiences brokenness, loses jobs, spouses, and health.

Addicted people need to find the motivation, force, and thirst for joy in living. The addict needs to attach to a Person. Addiction gives our lives over to the predicament of squalid misery and pain. Addicts and the mentally ill are outcasts from society. Bodily pleasures end in unhappiness and pain and finally early death. All that can change when any person encounters Jesus and finds not just pleasure but abundant life.

Preaching from the Word of God causes people to look at what God is doing in their lives. What is happening? Look at who you are. Some ministers, even professors of preaching believe that a preacher should never give a personal illustration about who we are or for illuminating an understanding of the scriptures. Preaching is in some ways a personal testimony. Fred Craddock also tells us something about himself in nearly every sermon. David Buttrick, who taught preaching at Vanderbilt, insisted that no minister should ever give a personal illustration. Personal stories distract many in the congregation. Stories in your personal life may have happened to you, but the event is not about you.

The Joy of Preaching

Ministers may be tempted to make themselves heroes or to create depreciation of themselves. Norman Vincent Peale was successful in his own style.

One thing we do know from experience is to not use our wives or children in our personal stories. Your loved ones may not appreciate it and they often remember the stories differently than you do. Ministers do need to examine their motives for using autobiography in their sermons.

The Word of God sometimes causes people to want to go back to Egypt. Obeying the Word is filled with risk and it is never easy to become converted and to repent of our old ways and playgrounds. The Hebrew people said to their leader Moses, "We would rather live in the slavery of Egypt than to trust God's Word that we can be free people."

People who place themselves on the throne of life do not care that the Word of God must be shared beyond the perceived exclusive church body.

Self-satisfied and unmoved people want the preacher to challenge them with no more than what that preacher reads from a magazine, a self-help book, or radio and television.

By taking authority in the pulpit, the preacher is obliged to preach the Word of God. He is called to share Christ the Person rather than sharing nice, intelligent words that please rebellious congregations, but not God.

Once a church member said to me, "Some in the congregation do not like your preaching. They just are not pleased." I think I said something like, "Well, I am not here to please them, but to please God." That might not get you anywhere!

Going back to Egypt often means doing the "proper" things in church rituals, energy to maintain the buildings, ministry to members only, worship in a tradition way, songs that entertain and sooth certain age groups. Back to Egypt might mean calling a pastor who preaches fire and brimstone, judging and condemning others who do not agree with their interpretations of God's Word.

Life is the preacher's library. The measure for success is how accessible is the Word of God to the audience. Churches whose pastors "go back to Egypt" find it really wasn't as pleasant as we might have thought. Dare to use the insights of scholarship and creativity. A student in one of my preaching classes created wonderful sermons using modern communication techniques. During the class where students preached their sermons for evaluation, one student said, "He'd never get by with preaching that in most congregations."

The Joy of Preaching

The preacher must choose his battles carefully, weighing whether igniting potential brush fires will jeopardize the quest for higher ground.

Safe preaching may not be faithful preaching. If Jesus had colored within the lines, imagine how differently his ministry would have been. Sermons that comfort rarely confront, and sermons that confront rarely comfort. Comfortable congregations are stagnant congregations. We all get our share of unjust and just criticism.

The Promised Land can only be found by embracing

God's gifts and creating an atmosphere where joy and miracles happen. A missionary congregation doesn't say, "What an excellent sermon," but they say with experience, "What a great God we have." That's the joy of preaching.

Chapter 7
The Way of the Cross Leads Home

ANOTHER YEAR, ANOTHER YEAR OF PREACHING the Word of God comes softy as Carl Sandburg said, "on little cat's feet." When we read of the horrible things that preachers in the New Testament or in our own day are plagued with, one ponders, why do it? Why preach? Why listen?

Some ministers are like the Beatles' Father McKenzie who is busy writing sermons "no one would hear." Week after week preachers attempt to compose something good. Poor messengers ignore the changes in life instead just speak as usual. Perhaps such sermons aim at solving problems, even spiritual ones.

Some do it because they are paid more than the average person. But that compensation comes to only a few. Most serve for

The Joy of Preaching

nothing but the joy of presenting Jesus. Business owners, lawyers, politicians, physicians, and engineers have more prestige and human honors than those God has called to preach.

So why do it? We do it because it is God who communicates through us. Paul urged Timothy in his final words to him, "Preach the Word." The Word of God is the exclusive tested fuel for the fire of our walk with Jesus through whom we have a relationship with the Father. We preach because it is an act of service to God and to others. It is our spiritual gift for the body of Christ.

We preach to introduce Jesus as Christ for others. Also, our preaching brings Good News that we can be restored and rescued as fallen creatures. We enable people to know what God is like. We do that by an encounter with Jesus in every sermon.

The way of Christ leads to the cross. The cross is clearly visible on the tops of church buildings, in our sanctuaries, and as a symbol with our vestments worn in worship.

The mystery at work in the preaching of the Good News is that as we take up the cross of Christ, we are in the way of eternal life. As the hymn says, "The way of the cross leads home."

Most of us called to preach are so naïve to think that the way of the cross is traveled without pain or struggle. After years of doing it, they learn that the cross is a small price to pay for the splendor of the risen life. We must die to ourselves.

We share in the resurrection. So we receive the cross with smiles on our faces and with happy tears because we have come to recognize that cross as the way that will bring us to our greatest joys.

It is not whether the called preacher will have a cross, but how the cross will be taken up in the unique contexts of our lives. The gift of preaching done for and in the body of Christ, the church, is never as glamorous as one may think. Jesus told us that they hated me, so they will hate you.

Jesus preaching led to his cross, so will be the preaching of all who follow him. Authentic communicators of the Word of God must be aware of the responses of those who hear us. Prayer and continuous reflection creates the mindfulness needed. The more fully alive preachers give themselves up to the sacrifices required by this ministry, the more open they become to the irrevocable joy to which taking up the cross leads us.

The cross of having to present something really good regardless of what weather conditions in hot summer or cold winter. Personal feelings, support of immediate family, or any difficulties may be in our way, but we must deliver on time.

The time for preaching comes despite lack of our current motivation or creativity. The times comes when we have so much material to share that we pare down and eliminate enough to be more effective. The time comes when we have nothing new to share. Ideas are scarce.

Nothing comes as with writer's block, but the preacher may search for hours for some small biblical nugget that will tide the people over until ideas become bountiful again.

At those times, preachers pray, "Lord Jesus, you get up there with me as I preach. May I say just what you would want to say to your children today?"

Preachers who are called or appointed to resourceful congregations take a sabbatical or vacation to renew and refresh themselves. Most never enjoy that blessing.

Preachers who put their heart and soul into their preaching are exhausted on Sunday afternoons. Some preach again on Sunday nights or in assisted living centers, jails, or hospitals every day. Most are exhausted. Most people who do not preach, do not understand how exhausting it is to carry this cross. Preachers do become weary to the point of mental and physical exhaustion from bearing this heavy cross.

If you continue to preach, and for some us it is not a long time from now, you will say or do something downright stupid.

James McReynolds

One preacher said in his message, "The sweetest, most beautiful woman I have ever held in my arms was another man's wife." The congregation sat in confused silence.

The minister continued, "She was my mother." Smiles of joy broke out on the congregation's faces.

Taking up the task of preaching leads to humiliating moments. Sometimes our anger, guilt, anxiety, or fear bleed out of us as we preach with passion and intensity.

Sometimes people want to hear the platform of their political party and not the Word of God. They may get the message, but they don't like it. So we get icy stares, angry glares, and silent airs, and they exit the building in another place. Some lecture us as others who are waiting to greet us look on. Some listen to hear us make a mistake.

Hate messages appear on our answer machines. Sometimes we get wrathful phone calls. Preachers are ridiculed and humiliated. It hurts to hear ugly criticism or condemning words from outside, but the most hurtful pain comes from the members of our own congregations.

Often babies cry, old folks cough as we try so hard to give the message that has taken hours to prepare. Sometimes a church will not grow. Pastors say that they'll never serve a dead congregation, yet the reality is that some churches must just close. They are now in a dying cycle. No matter who the pastor is, no one can change a town with too many churches, a village that is losing its population, or a church that has been ruled by a few people.

Preachers must bear the cross of loneliness. Being a preacher turns us into someone who is kind of odd. Compared to the number of people who are members of churches, those who regularly stand up to the microphone to preach the Word of God are relatively few. During counseling sessions with persons addicted to drugs, angry people, or folks in life pain, I hear cuss words or disrespectful language. Then the person will say, "Oh, I apologize preacher. That's just my way."

Laughter and foul language stops when I give a spirituality lecture in an addictions center or in a prison. Preachers are freakish to those who do not believe the gospel.

Some even think preachers do not have sex or passion. They say that there are males, females, and preachers.

Saint Paul wrote that "preaching was foolishness" to those who do not believe. So the preacher is thought of as a fool.

Peter and Paul suffered because they preached so people encountered Jesus, and reject him and the apostles. They were beaten, imprisoned, brought before secular and religious councils, and ridiculed. As we know Jesus, we anticipate that some of these experiences will be ours as our cross to bear.

James McReynolds

No preacher is exempt from hard work, humiliation, disappointment, or loneliness. We lose church members, spouses, children, money, and health to preach the Word as did Jesus whose gospel we preach.

We bear our crosses because in this way we unite ourselves with Jesus. We are his voice, his body, his work. So we are mystically united with others who preach. Called preachers share a deep bond. At convocations, meetings, and clergy groups, we are bound up with others who make up Christ's body.

The ministry of preaching is not easy for anyone. Some dread preparing a message on a regular basis. Some just quit. Some people can sit in silence as they read, think, and compose on a computer. Using words comes naturally to me. I enjoy creating newsletters, books, articles, radio and television programs, and making tapes to share my messages throughout the world.

Like many serious preachers, I feel much anxiety as I preach. I always have. I was anxious as a 12-year old giving his first sermon. And I am just as anxious after 60 years in the preaching ministry.

My anxiety increases when I think I have something to say worth listening to. I have joy during the delivery. After the presentation I am drained. I then breathe a sigh of relief. It is finished. And so am I.

The Joy of Preaching

Being a preacher means taking up a cross of sacrifice. We give up our lives in ways others would not do. Often, my family goes on vacation or to a fun event, but I can't go with them. Many times, especially Sundays, my wife or family and friends have to wait an hour or so while I shut down and recharge my human batteries. I hate not having enough energy to do things I must do.

The cross of sacrifice forces the clergy person to have the family embrace that cross also. Sometimes the union between Christ Jesus and me gives me moments of joy. Keeping aware of those joy times gives my life meaning and purpose.

"The way of the cross" leads us to places we would not consider as where we would serve. "Everything happens for a reason," my mother used to say. She was correct.

Now that I look back on seven decades of life, I can now discern that "all things work together for good to those called unto God's purposes." The right place is here. The time is now.

Where we are born, who we marry, where we go to school, where we travel, what our gifts and talents are, who influences us, and everything we encounter can work together for good, as "the way of the cross leads home."

When we go to heaven, we might be asked, "Did you enjoy your journey through the world?"

James McReynolds

Dying on your personal cross will save nobody. Jesus did that already. We will come closer to fulfilling our purpose in life by working less. Feel the joy of a movie or a play as you say grace for the privilege. My wife recently bought a big tub of popcorn and a large soda just because she had never done that before. Play cards with your church members. Go bowling. One of my joys as a pastor of the First Baptist Church in Hallsville, Missouri was to play dominoes with "Granny" Norris.

We are moving toward a crisis in preaching in Europe and in North America. In my world travels to share preaching Vision quests for Christ, I have found greater passion for Jesus in Asia, Africa, and South America than in many congregations in the United States. The cross of preaching gets heavier every day.

Effective preaching takes both time and risk and courage. It does not always require polish or education or eloquence.

Dan Graham, the old-time preacher in Bristol, Tennessee, told me before I entered Carson-Newman College that education was a waste of time. I had been preaching for about six years before going to college. My freshman year at Carson-Newman, I went for almost 200 days before I was asked to preach. Dan Taylor, the Greek professor at Carson-Newman, was to preach one Sunday, but after seeing me after a spiritual direction session, he told the church that I would be speaking in a Baptist church in Jefferson City in his stead.

Becoming more skillful through education sets us up for unfair and unnecessary comparison. Also, it is an illusion that effective sermons are produced by experts with professional degrees instead of humble people who are willing to spend all their waking hours fighting the same demons and angels that the congregation does every day.

Preachers are human. The cross for preachers from within and without is to be more human, to show the wounds.

Within the membership are those who hide their beer or vodka from the pastor, act like they are seeing a scandal brewing if we run with our shorts on through the neighborhood, or if we go into a bar to connect with somebody who needs to talk to us about relapsing from addiction.

Ministers need a hands-on experience of the human condition and willingness to speak about it. Some Nebraska pastors spend a week in downtown Omaha serving the homeless, visiting places where addicts and hurting criminals live in abundance. They call the week an "Urban Plunge." Perhaps preaching of the Word of God would be better after one has had that kind of experience.

Share yourself and be an ambassador for Christ. People come to church to hear you. They want the human voice that comes with your body, with being Christ to the desperate and the poor, the addict and the rich ones who have never known happiness.

James McReynolds

Preachers need to be human, to be naïve and vulnerable in public. If you don't speak to them from deep in your soul, in awareness of what matters to them, then who will? How can they hear the Word of God without a preacher?

Our journey of faith is in response to the call of Christ. When we let go of our old securities and embrace risk and hardship, we discover the sustaining presence of God in new and deeper ways. God is discovered afresh by our cross bearing experiences in life.

That's what the scripture means by "the joy of the cross." And that's the joy of preaching.

Chapter 8
Preaching Joy and the Coming Kingdom

PREACHING IS SUCH A POWERFUL WAY TO REACH into the hearts of God's children to give them "the joy of the Lord." One of my former church members wrote that he had hit his bottom in his life struggle with drugs and alcohol. He said that he found "strength" and "comfort" from a sermon he had heard me preach twenty years ago. His story was proof to me that the Word of God is never void.

He is now happily sober. He does odd jobs and sings in the church choir in a congregation which he joined after Jesus rescued him from that bottom.

Preaching brings people back to life. Preaching really does renew us. By seeing how others are made new, we will find our joyful call enlivened to preach more creative sermons. God is always at work in us offering personal renewal as we are refueled by the Holy Spirit.

How can we be ready in season and out of season? Some weeks we just cannot come up with that "something good." Perhaps someone in your family got sick. Maybe you prepared for a funeral. Perhaps you composed a graduation speech for a baccalaureate. I know how honored I am to preach a sermon to support the young people on a special time in their life journey. I preached my first one for graduates of Hallsville High School in Hallsville, Missouri. I've given 87 baccalaureate sermons for religious and secular schools.

Despite our current interpretation of laws about separation of church and state, pastors continue to speak in a community school, if it is student initiated.

Every week there is some human crisis for which has not been scheduled by anyone. In March 2013, a basketball mounted goal fell into a crowd during a sports event. The school needed a message about God's love and accidents which come to the just and the unjust. That week most pastors in Weeping Water used illustrations to comfort the people.

The spiritual gift of preaching is just that, a gift from God. So we thank the giver by enjoying the gift. Preaching enables people to expect joys in life with an overall happy attitude of happiness

The Joy of Preaching

despite all the struggles that are faced. The Word of God gives strength and reason for the countless compromises and concessions that we have settled for in our days on earth. They need a reason to believe and trust.

Focus on the pleasures for the body such as sins that give "pleasure for a season," but in the end give death and pain, anger and disappointment, guilt and loss, fear and mistrust.

Good preaching gives that reason to let go of the past and to encounter Jesus who creates in them an abundant life where they are right this moment.

Our purpose in preaching is clear: to guide us all in achieving union with God and living as people who are members of the kingdom of God. One's preaching takes a comprehensive look at how we can be transformed as individuals, as a church assembly, as a denomination, and to have the power of the Holy Spirit to serve Jesus Christ in the world, to the end that God is glorified and souls are transformed from a spiritual death as we live on earth and in the next world.

The kingdom of God was the heart of Jesus' ministry. He continued to have this kingdom life which he preached even after his resurrection. (Acts 1:1-3) After the resurrection, his time was limited. So Jesus used the time wisely to explain the features of the kingdom. He knew that those called to communicate, in cooperation with the coming Holy Spirit as members of the Body of Christ, needed to be clear about what to preach and teach. The future of the Kingdom and the Church depended on these men and women knowing the essentials for living in that kingdom. The kingdom is now here in an embryonic way. It will be totally fulfilled and established with the return of Jesus. The Kingdom of God is the visible presence of the Church, the body of Christ. (Luke 17:20-21)

Effective preaching is done by one who realizes that the Kingdom of God contains all the elements of the Christian gospel. Every other message that we share is simply commentary on the kingdom. The goal is to have God through Jesus and his Holy Spirit to reign in our hearts, minds, and souls.

So we say with our Lord Jesus we must preach the kingdom of God because that is the purpose of our call. Transformed congregations come to see that happiness is the inner realization that we are loved by God.

Good preaching tells people who they are. It gives them back the humanity that God intended for them before they were born. The world keeps people in a state of spiritual amnesia. Trusting Jesus makes much more sense than all those ungodly arguments of the people who keep on trusting their addictions. Jesus makes all the difference. Good preaching gives people the right to hope. Preaching removes our pity for self and our nothingness. Good preaching causes us to find a reason to eagerly live the rest of their lives.

Whenever we share the happiness that we have found through Jesus our words become an attraction to others. Preaching with skill as a wordsmith and with confident passion gives the reason that people not give up on their quest for happiness.

Natural gifts must be supported by grace. That precious humble reality causes us to work hard will cause your God-given talents to increase with the pain you take. Nothing good will come without work.

Jesus will come with us into the pulpit. Christ prays for us and for those who will come to believe because of our words that become Jesus' words and the Word of God.

When a congregation looks into the eyes of their preacher, they will see the burning rays of beauty in Jesus. They will come to know personally just who the Christ is. They will risk their lives on Jesus' promises.

God uses preaching as the instrument to break the power of evil. Preaching is God's weapon for light to reign over darkness. The devil has no power strong enough to stop the Word of God from overcoming the world. We embrace the cross of preaching because it releases captives and the resurrection of the dead. The words we craft are the words that ensure the ultimate fulfillment of our constant prayer:

> "Thy kingdom come, thy will be done on earth as it is in Heaven."

Revelation is a book that says the Lamb of God will win in the end. In this book, often the source of bad preaching which serves self and gives no joyful interpretation or hope.

In Revelation 19:15, Jesus is described as wearing a robe which has been dipped in blood. He is named "the Word of God." John the Revelator goes on to write, "From his mouth comes a sharp sword with which to strike down the nations." The Word of God as the Bible tells us is the sharp two-edged sword that proceeds from the mouth of Christ.

The coming kingdom of God results from the response to preaching the Word of God. Good preaching day by day, week by week, year by year will shake the congregation out of lethargy, out from depression, out from negativity, out of temptation, and inspired to be part of the body of Christ.

I treasure letters, cards, and emails from someone who was blessed through my preaching. God spoke to them in a personal way.

The Joy of Preaching

Sometimes a person will return to active participation in their local church and to begin to perceive it as the eternal part of the kingdom of God. Sometimes an addict finds the courage to seek counseling after a lifetime of denial. Preaching encourages people to forgive long past hurts. When these things happen, God is glorified and my human reaction is irrevocable joy.

To serve a congregation well, you need to withdraw from them from time to time. You do have to decide for yourself what will meet your needs. Starving souls produce really bad messages. Some of us are revived by solitude while others thrive on human company. Nobody can give you the right solution for meeting your needs. I know from decades of preaching that we need to do something different to plump up our souls and give balance to our lives.

To protect your time for preparing sermons, you have to just take it. The same goes for prayer, being intimate with your family, resting, and "having a life."

Many preachers live beyond the biblical three scores and ten. Your earthy life is a precious gift. Preachers must be enlivened to know life more abundant. Life is more important than religion.

Kingdom life is about God and community. The gathered fellowship of the church here on earth is a foretaste, an anticipation of the kingdom of God. Every time we gather as a church, the body of Christ, we anticipate the feast of the kingdom at the end of time. How are we to "do" church?

How do we live our lives in this world of need where people are poor, crippled, lame, and blind?

Our churches ought to be a kingdom party, the ultimate feast of the kingdom of God. Hospitality is extended to all. The needy are invited and that means all of us who have responded to the Word of God in our encounter with Jesus.

And that's the joy of preaching.

Chapter 9
Preaching and the Conversion of the Soul

One old time preacher that I admired was Dan Graham, a Presbyterian pastor from the seat of Sullivan County in Blountville, Tennessee. He preached many revivals throughout town and country in East Tennessee and Southwest Virginia. He often said that the only reason for preaching was the conversion of souls.

Graham was a stance fundamentalist. He spoke of the sins of movie going, card playing, mixed bathing, drinking, smoking, cussing, or irreverence of any kind. My mother told me that once when Graham was preaching on the radio, she felt so guilty about having shorts on that she changed into a dress.

James McReynolds

The central interest in preaching correlates to an impulse inside our human condition, namely the search for a meaning in life. It is natural to belong to God.

Why do people come to church and hear preaching? What are we looking for? Why did thousands of people go inside a tent or a brush arbor to hear Dan Graham? Why did they drive thousands of miles to hear Billy Graham? What were they looking for? They did not spend their time to merely get some knowledge or to exchange some ideas.

Today we can receive information or ideas from the Internet. We can find much easier, comprehensive, and convenient ways of getting data we need about God and faith than from words from a pulpit.

So why do we need preaching? Because preaching the Word of God is a personal encounter with God himself. That word can change lives. We embrace God's Word in experiencing a living presence. People are moved by the Holy Spirit as the Word of God enters one's soul. This event is not an emotional or sentimental thing. We find in faith, a reason, and a purpose to live. What we need to be fully the person God created us to be, we do not automatically have inside us.

We can never conjure it up or find it by ourselves. Life must be given to us from outside. We put ourselves before a preacher filled with the expectation that it will be given to us to discover all we need to be ourselves. We hear the Word of God to become more complete, finding the meaning and purpose of our journey receiving a new power and optimism. We must go to the event of preaching to be changed, revived, repaired, recharged, and restored. That is, we respond to the Word of God with a mysterious conversion to be lived.

Sin indeed has made us and God unhappy. God desires nothing more than our times of joy and overall happiness despite the guilt, the anger, anxiety, and fear that must be converted.

Jesus came preaching and healing. His preaching illustrated the healings. "Salvus" in Latin means "health."

It is the root for the word salvation. The Twelve Step program called it "recovery." Too many members of our Recovery groups settle for more sobriety from drugs instead of a real transforming of the self. So they go on waiting for death instead of enjoying God's joy banquet much earlier in life.

One of the transforming ministries we have used at the First Christian Church in Weeping Water is a support group for those living with addictions that is called Recovery. In defining our Higher Power, we use God in Jesus Christ, not just a group, an impersonal religion, a dead family member, or some other reality.

Recovery makes practical the same teachings that Jesus gave us, but without the clumsy spiritualizing that gives room for opinion, obstinacy, and open rebellion against the taking God within us through Jesus which has the power to convert us and the earth. In endless arguing about spirituality, we avoid both body and soul. So addicted humans suffer the consequences of a body addicted as well as a soulless community.

To be converted is to encounter love that changes us within with other souls in an atmosphere of joy and love. Our deep longings are fulfilled, not because of our goodness but because of Jesus' goodness.

To experience conversion is to belong. We are never alone. Conversion rescues us from isolation, alienation, and loneliness. Now we are in a relationship with God who loves us. Life now has purpose and meaning. Changed from despair to hope, we are in the most reasonable position to hold as we face the world. We see ourselves as God sees us. Salvation means that we become like little children in order to enter the kingdom of God. Jesus commands us to be converted.

The assurance that our calling to preach can give the experience of conversion to others comes from the God who lives in us. When Jesus is preached, people are saved. When the rich young ruler rejected Jesus' offer to be saved from his possessions and greed, Jesus turns to those remaining who have accepted him, he says, "Children, how hard it is to enter the kingdom of God." (Mark 10:24) When we encounter Jesus through the Word of God we are radically changed and become like children. According to John's gospel, he gives us that power to become children of God.

The Samaritan woman at the well made a 180-degree change as she encounters Jesus. Even the exposure of her many sins cannot dull the freedom and new life she discovers in meeting Jesus. She leaves her old life and says to people, "Come see a man who told me all I ever did." So her moment of joy is something she cannot help but share with others.

Preaching keeps in mind what the community desires from life. Some want a second chance. None of their pleasures satisfy. They hear the Word of God to find the destiny that leads to happiness now and for all time. Jesus rescues us from the rubble of our lives. Preaching is a means of grace that causes grace. Being conformed to Christ, the preacher brings other souls to Jesus. People seek out the preacher who gave the words that changed their lives.

Peter wrote, "You have been born anew, not of perishable seed but from imperishable, through the living and abiding Word of God." (I Peter 1:23) The Bible gives help for every human experience. It gives meaning to an encounter with Jesus.

James McReynolds

No preaching can help save people unless the preacher is being saved. Salvation can happen quickly. My church often says, "What happened in the church last Sunday that so many received Christ?" What happened was the preaching of the Word and happenings like that will be experienced more often when our hearers encounter Jesus. After that our preaching must for them include discipleship for living in the mystery of living our days.

Chapter 10
Why Bother With Preaching in the Church Today?

IN MANY CHURCHES TODAY, PREACHING HAS GONE the way of prayer meeting, Sunday School, visitation, two week Vacation Bible Schools, and Sunday night worship.

Our churches are filled with biblically illiterate members. We don't even go to church if it is too hot or too cold, and when the weather is just right, we find something more vital to do even on the Lord's Day.

Given the current climate of organized religion, life in the United States has radically changed. The United States is no longer a

"Christian nation." We are not even a Judeo-Christian country. We are a multi-religious culture.

And we are not a print-based culture. People expect what is called contemporary music, five to eight minute sermons if they even choose to use a sermon. We now live with an electronic culture dominated by videos on a screen. There is rarely passionate proclamation, but more of instruction messages with no encounter with what to do with the message. Passionate preaching is not just a lecture on joy but a Word that produces joy.

We have examined the effect of the lectionary on preaching. Southern Baptists and a few other evangelicals have never adopted the lectionary. Some Episcopalians, United Methodists, Presbyterians, and Roman Catholics tend to do instruction preaching rather than proclamation or Word of God preaching centered proclamation. Lectionary preachers tend to like summary resolution texts. Some avoid soul issues.

They leave out the troubling, difficult issues, so that hearers are not bothered with problems, conversion, or repentance. Preaching a sermon is not equal or the same thing as an essay. It is no wonder that people are leaving some traditional mainline churches.

Good preachers spend more time in study than any other profession. Tuition for four years of college and six or seven years of seminary for a doctoral degree is more than the average parishioner can imagine. Why?

People want a reason to find something beyond the compromising life. They need reasons for believing. They need something that is really healthy. One of my colleagues in divinity school said that preaching is important because it enables the human soul to rise to the hope and joys of heaven. In simpler words, people face problems in living every day. They feel utterly powerless. They will not give up on life, but on their own they cannot solve the problem.

They come to worship wanting to hear a Word that will make life different. They know they need a new perspective. They kept doing the same things but life just gets more complicated.

Going inside a church and hearing a preacher gives them some relief. The prepared message seems to be words addressed just to them. This is really why we still have preaching in church.

Preaching never was about information. The Word of God contains and communicates a reason. Preaching is a mysterious means of grace that quickens strength and resolve so we can go on. This is another reason we keep having sermons preached during worship.

Most ministerial students take speech classes in college. Preaching a sermon is not the same as giving a speech. Nobody has ever been converted by a message. If so, then God might have chosen to deliver a message rather than sending his Son to speak to the world personally. Socrates, Ovid, and others have given messages to the world, including multitudes of prophets, visionaries, and teachers. Despite all that people are more confused, miserable, addictive, and prone to malice, negative, cynical, lonely, afraid, and lost than at any other time in history. More than just a good teacher is required. So it is not a problem solving tool, but a mystery in an encounter with a powerful person.

People are in deep pain. The Church must give a healing message filled with love. Doubt, despair, and lack of resources crowd in upon life. Jesus is an attractive alternative. More people today find preaching to be boring. People will listen to the words of preaching if it is pertinent to living, even important as a life or death experience. To encounter the living Jesus is to know the sermon will enrich and delight us in our souls.

Why bother with preaching? People in our day have decided to depose God and put themselves in his place. So preaching must face an impossible impasse. So these souls dismiss preaching as a foolish, futile, fatuous exercise. People are caught up in sin. Yet they sense nothing of personal awareness of encountering God. Many things about ourselves cannot be changed. So it is natural to ask: Who made me? Why do I exist? Someone decided to place us in this world. What is my mission on this planet?

The Joy of Preaching

Our desires are leading us somewhere. Can we trust our desires? Will some Higher Power give me satisfaction for my desires? Desires suggest some big plan and they make me eager to go after it. Will my desires lead me to my Maker? Our limitations cause us to depend on something unlimited.

So the unlimited God is who has the ability and desire to help us. The Holy Spirit will actually come to our assistance and rescue us in response to our seeking. So our experience of limitation enables us to be believers that our Creator is overseeing the whole of my life. Something inside of us causes us to want to know what happiness looks like. It looks a lot like Jesus whom we encounter in preaching the Word of God. We feel cheated if we do not have happiness in our lives. Preachers give the Word for both rich and poor. Some have many things the world can offer: money, family, freedom, friends, but they all seek happiness. Preaching helps us at least to see what happiness looks like and how it can become a habit and unhappiness will feel foreign. People do have a narrow definition, thinking it means a good mood or experiencing the emotion joy all the time. That's impossible.

It is the counterfeit Christian preacher who thinks joy is happiness. Happiness is a way of life, an overriding outlook composed of qualities such as love, fulfillment, courage, love, and optimism. Carnal, sinful people have lost their love for life. Fear keep coming up, but encountering Jesus helps us make our way out of darkness of our past into the light of today.

James McReynolds

I wrote my books on joy from researching and studying about joy at Vanderbilt Divinity School and Oxford University. Healthy people know what joy looks like. I enjoy giving seminars and retreats, revivals and workshops on the human emotion joy. It is a key for identifying a kingdom person.

Preaching is one kind of communication, but so is counseling individuals, writing books and articles, media, newsletters, teaching, or sending letters. I am a licensed mental health practitioner and thus have another tool to help people to solve and accept problems. Pastoral psychotherapy helps people understand their fears.

It helps people lay off drugs and alcohol, not just by forbidding them, but by healing the pain in the soul that drugs were used to soothe. Pleasure is uniquely effective at masking fear.

Even Jesus provided the pleasure of drinking wine during a wedding celebration. Happy people celebrate small achievements, such as finishing a day's work. Most pleasure is used in celebration such as using wine, dancing, music, feasting, stories, and sex. During these pleasure events, people forget their fears and worries. They relax and recharge their batteries. Pleasures are for happy people the punctuation marks of living. Those unhappy souls stay too long at a party and end up celebrating celebration. Returning to normal life, they are filled with guilt, toxicity, and more pronounced physical addiction.

The Joy of Preaching

Addicts can never overcome their weaknesses without help. Sometimes I preach on the Twelve Steps from the Word of God. Everyone has some kind of addiction.

When I deliver spirituality lectures for treatment centers, listeners will sometimes clap, responding to my lecture as something really fresh and new. Some even say they enjoyed my "sermon," although I did not intend to be preaching.

All of us have an innate need and expectation for happiness. Left to ourselves, we have no tools for the fullness we need. And our experiences tell us that the only thing that will fulfill my soul is not a thing. It is a Person.

One purpose of preaching is to activate and educate a person's spirituality. When our spirituality is awakened and enlivened, we pray as the Psalmist, "Bow your heavens, O Lord, and come down." (Psalm 144:5) And the mysterious reality is that God does just that. Becoming aware of what Jesus means first becoming aware of the nature of what makes a person human. Accepting Jesus opens up our souls to admire, thank, acknowledge, and live in Jesus the Christ.

Preachers activate the spirituality of others only if he is alert and sensitive to the urging of spirituality in his own life.

Preaching is about reconciliation. Souls have been broken by sin. So they choose to distract, encrust, anesthetize, and repress awareness. Some say that they have traded in religion for spirituality. Some of those who are convinced their way of spirituality avoid old traditions and the way church people divide people from one another. They need truly happy congregations that enable people to encounter Jesus and to practice faith, not just a certain set of beliefs which offers a vague universalism that says all of us are the same or an airtight unyielding creed that leaves many people out.

Preaching is the method God has called us for people in the grip of sin an opportunity to be born again from above. The Word answers a lived question in hearers. The genius of the Bible is that it offers not simply a message but a divine, life-giving presence. With knowledge of God and his ways, the preacher must pass on that knowledge as one with a living experience of the mystery of sharing the Word.

Why preaching? In our town kids are required to play sports games, the adults read the newspaper, go to the home show convention, visits relatives, go to brunch, or just sleep in on Sundays. Writing the history of preaching each historian writes about the "golden age of preaching." The golden age is always at least three or four generations ago.

There has always been good preaching. Of course in every era, the excellence ones are few and far between. There are more conclusions about the poor health of preaching than in any other age. People who attend church on a regular basis wonder why people who attend a divinity school such as Yale, Harvard, Vanderbilt, and the denominational seminaries are not better at preaching. Preachers are hard on themselves. Most who know they are called to preach want to be better.

So why bother with preaching? So we encounter Jesus and find personal salvation. Will that change the social order? People who claim to be born again are counterfeit in that they support the culture. Preaching the Word or encountering Jesus means to reflect on what Jesus taught and preached in his day. We must be careful not to worship and preach on the Bible as the Book and not Jesus as the one offering our redemption.

God is at the center, not the local congregation. The missionary church opens people from inward concerns to outward looking ones. Maintenance centered congregations can center on who is wrong and who is right.

Who has the authority? Loving one another is more important than how we express our beliefs. Thus we become peace makers, life savers, and joy producers, not just gatekeepers for dying traditions.

When I was ordained as an elder in the United Methodist Church, the bishop said, "Take thou authority." The call to serve is prompted by the living God. Authority, especially the authority to preach, is not conferred by any church or denominated body, nor is it based on one's accomplishments.

Why do we preach? Because God called us to share what we have experienced in Jesus and in our journey throughout our lives, we need preaching in the church today.

Preaching is not about us, but it centers on the encounter with Jesus the Christ. We will never be perfect preachers.

Trying to be perfect keeps the Word of God from saving us to new life. Preaching that centers on any preacher shines too much light on the person or the performance. Why bother to have preaching? If it is used to keep people in line, petty problem solving, proper lectionary explanation, entertainment, or trivial "sounds of fury signifying nothing," then this is not a means of grace and is practically useless.

We must not compare ourselves with other preachers. Comparisons are the indoor sport of preachers. Paul wrote in II Corinthians 10:12 that when we measure ourselves by ourselves and compare ourselves with ourselves, we are wise." We are not in competition with other preachers. We are only in competition with ourselves. By God's grace, we ought to be better preachers and pastors today that we were a year ago. The so-called giants among preachers were all hard workers.

If God has called us, then God will give you what you need to do your spiritual gift. We may not have gifts that other servants have, or all you wish we had, but God gives you that which the Lord needs for us to have.

Discover and develop your gift. Do not be discouraged that some people would just as soon not have preaching in worship.

Whatever your handicaps may be, let God make use of them and everything you are. God did miracles with the apostle Paul with his thorn in the flesh. Preaching is not so much what we do in the body of Christ, but what we are. God knew us before we were born. Our Maker knows us better than we know ourselves. All the experiences we preachers go through are not accidents, they are appointments.

God makes sure that many events or people will come our way that we cannot manage on our own. People who move from one success to another seeming success seldom understand success at all, except a limited version. People who are humble and faithful with God's mysterious help break through with love and joy to find their purpose and meaning.

Preaching the Word is not a moral issue that we do not desire. Maybe some Christians desire to worship without a message because it asks nothing of them personally.

James McReynolds

To find our purpose in the body of Christ, our hearts need to be broken to have a heart for others. Salvation is not just an evacuation plan for the next world. Few congregations believe in what the Word offers in the Revelation of John. Salvation offers us a new heaven and a new earth. (Revelation 21:1)

Encountering the living Christ really does save us. It is beyond what we ever imagined or earned by ourselves. As long as the spiritual journey is viewed as a moral achievement contest, none of us will ever feel worthy, ready, or able to let go of control of our lives.

The accepted reality is that people sleep through sermons. Recently I went to a hospital to have people watch me sleep. That test determined whether I lived with sleep apnea. Those who preach have watched people sleep for many years as we give our sermons. During that hospital test, people were watching me.

Not everyone slumbers while we preach, and hearers laugh as they hear a snore from bored people. Some can doze with their eyes open. They don't expect much because there is so little newsworthy about what we say. Newspapers used to use entire sermons as news. People grabbed the first edition of the London Times to read or re-read the preaching event given by Spurgeon. Billy Graham's sermons were printed in the Los Angeles Times as the publisher, William Randolph Hurst told his newspapers "to

The Joy of Preaching

puff Graham." Perhaps Graham would not be known today if the powerful media industry did not push him into the limelight.

It is quite natural for ministers to preach in ways that build up the local church. That kind of word suggests that only those inside the church building perceive all things correctly, for example, that the goal of God is to get the people in the world to come into the church. God's goal in reading of the gospel is to bring the church into the world, to put the followers of Jesus at the service of all God's other children, until love has time to regenerate their hearts. That kind of faith and commitment brings not just security and safety, but a promise of painful transformation, sacrifice, and tension with the world.

Scripture holds truths which transcend antiquated language. The Bible is pertinent to us today. Many of our old and news church members rarely use words like atonement, propitiation, or sacramental. The preacher is the translator, translating accurately, without cluttering the way. The Word of God is the message. The preacher is merely the medium.

Preaching causes people to be aware that something is happening in our midst. Mysteriously Jesus has come preaching through somebody human called to proclaim that we are now free. We do not have to live the old way anymore.

James McReynolds

With Jesus inside us we really do come alive again. That's why we bother with preaching in our congregations today.

Some Resources for Preaching

The day one earns a doctorate degree in any field is not the end but the beginning. I have read thousands of books over the years to help me to continue to be the best servant of my Lord that I can be.

Some resources that I have been guided by include anything by my Vanderbilt professor Dr. John Killinger.

Fred Craddock's book *Preaching* (Nashville: Abingdon Press, 1985) is filled with practical wisdom. R.E.C. Browne's work, *The Ministry of the Word* (Philadelphia: Fortress Press, 1976)helps keep me fresh.

Commentaries that I use include those from many denominational press publishers to get a wider view. Each year I attend seminars and workshops on preaching at various seminaries. John Knox Press published a good commentary *Interpretation*. Books and

James McReynolds

lecture tapes on the Old and New Testaments by Amy-Jill Levine, a Jewish professor of New Testament at Vanderbilt, was a must for me.

Yngve Brilioth's small book, *A Brief History of Preaching,* is a good one for keeping preaching in historical perception.

I enjoyed *Twenty Centuries of Great Preaching* in 13 volumes, edited by Clyde Fant, Southern Baptist, and William Pinson, Methodist, published in Waco, Texas by Word Press in 1971.

I like Abingdon Press's *Preaching the New Common Lectionary.* It comes out in three volumes each year.

Life is the main resource. Talk to people. Hear their stories. Read newspapers and magazines, novels and great literature.

About the Author

THE REV. DR. JAMES MCREYNOLDS CELEBRATES his Diamond Jubilee 60th anniversary as a preacher with this book.

Norman Vincent Peale declared, "Your preaching embraced with joy, will be, as my positive thinking, a fresh vision for communicating Christian faith. Jim, I anoint you minister of joy to the world." His professor of preaching wrote, "I'm very proud of you, Jim. You've fulfilled Norman V. Peale's blessing for you, that you would be the minister of joy. You've made the world a better place."

He has preached in virtually every nation in the world. Millions have read his books, printed sermons, and newsletters. Others have listened to him on radio and television.

Jim's education includes a degree in English from Carson-Newman University; a degree in journalism from the University of Missouri; a masters in religious education from Midwestern

James McReynolds

Baptist Theological Seminary; a doctor of psychology from the Graduate Theological Foundation including Notre Dame, Rome, and Oxford Universities; master of divinity and doctorate in preaching, worship, and literature from Vanderbilt Divinity School.

www.ingramcontent.com/pod-product-compliance
Lightning Source LLC
Chambersburg PA
CBHW071730090426
42738CB00011B/2440